Hello young explorers, history buffs, and curious minds! Welcome aboard "Unveiling the Titanic's Fascinating Facts for Kids," penned by your captain on this educational voyage, William Anchor. Are you ready to set sail into one of the most captivating tales in history? Strap on your life vests, because this is going to be an unforgettable journey.

You might have heard of the Titanic—the grand ship that was as magnificent as a palace, as mighty as a fortress, but met an unfortunate fate on its maiden voyage. Whether you're new to this tale or have dipped your toes into these icy waters before, this book is your treasure chest of Titanic facts, tales, and wonders.

Why should you read this book, you ask? Well, the Titanic isn't just a ship, it's a grand story that sails through engineering, human ambition, heroism, tragedy, and yes, lots of ice-cold water! You're not just learning about a shipwreck, you're uncovering life lessons, science, geography, technology, and so much more.

Most importantly, this book is specially designed for young learners like you. Whether you're looking for interesting topics for your school project, or simply curious about the world around you, this book aims to satisfy your thirst for knowledge. You'll find questions and answers that unravel the mysteries of the Titanic in a way that's fun, interactive, and easily digestible. So, no heavy reading—just a light, enjoyable dive into the depths of history.

So are you ready to unveil the secrets of the Titanic? Open the first chapter and start your adventure now. Ahoy, mateys!

Sincerely,

William Anchor

01
FAQ
THE SHIP'S BASICS

Q

Where was the Titanic built?

A

It was built in
Belfast, Northern Ireland

02

FAQ

THE SHIP'S BASICS

Q

How long did it take to build the Titanic?

A

About 3 years from 1909 to 1912

03
FAQ
THE SHIP'S BASICS

 **Q** How big was the Titanic?

A The Titanic was about as long as three football fields put together!

04

FAQ

THE SHIP'S BASICS

Q

How many people helped
build the Titanic?

A

Over 15,000 people were
involved in building this
magnificent ship.

05

FAQ

THE SHIP'S BASICS

Q How much did a first-class ticket on the Titanic cost?

A A first-class ticket could cost up to $4,350, which is equivalent to about $100,000 today!

06

FAQ

THE SHIP'S BASICS

Q How big was the Titanic's anchor?

A The anchor weighed 15.5 tons and needed 20 horses to transport it.

07
FAQ

Q How many people could the Titanic's Grand Staircase hold?

A The Grand Staircase was so large that it could fit the entire population of a small village—about 100 people could comfortably stand on it at the same time.

08

FAQ

THE SHIP'S BASICS

Q How much coal did the Titanic use every day?

A

The ship burned around 600 tons of coal per day, shoveled by a team of 176 men!

09
FAQ
THE SHIP'S BASICS

 **Q**

How old is the Titanic?

 **A**

As of 2023, the Titanic would be 111 years old

10

FAQ

THE CONSTRUCTION AND DESIGN

Q What kind of wood was used in the interiors?

A Mahogany and oak were commonly used for the luxurious interiors

11
FAQ

THE CONSTRUCTION AND DESIGN

 Who designed the Titanic?

Thomas Andrews was the chief designer

12

FAQ

THE CONSTRUCTION AND DESIGN

Q How much did the Titanic cost to build?

A It cost about $7.5 million at that time, which is equivalent to around $180 million today.

13
FAQ

THE CONSTRUCTION AND DESIGN

Q

What made the Titanic considered 'unsinkable'?

A

It had watertight compartments, which unfortunately weren't enough.

14

FAQ

THE CONSTRUCTION AND DESIGN

Q How many propellers did the Titanic have?

A

It had three propellers

15

FAQ

THE CONSTRUCTION AND DESIGN

Q Were there any injuries or accidents during the construction?

A Unfortunately, yes. It's estimated that 246 injuries occurred and two workers died during the construction.

16

FAQ

THE CONSTRUCTION AND DESIGN

Q Was the Titanic the only ship of its kind?

A No, it had two sister ships: Britannic and Olympic. The Olympic was the only one that had a long service life.

17

FAQ

THE CONSTRUCTION AND DESIGN

Q How did they paint such a huge ship?

A It took 30 men nearly three years to paint the Titanic. They used 20,000 gallons of paint!

18
FAQ

PASSENGERS & CREW

 **How many classes of passengers were there?**

There were three: First, Second, and Third class.

19
FAQ
PASSENGERS & CREW

 **Q** Who was the captain of the Titanic?

A The captain was Edward Smith

20

FAQ

PASSENGERS & CREW

 **Q** Were there any famous people on the Titanic?

A Yes! One of them was John Jacob Astor IV, who was one of the richest men in the world at the time. He was traveling with his 19-year-old pregnant wife, Madeleine. Sadly, he didn't survive, but his wife did.

21

FAQ

THE ICEBERG & SINKING

What time did the Titanic hit the iceberg?

It hit the iceberg at 11:40 PM on April 14, 1912

22

FAQ

THE ICEBERG & SINKING

Q How long did it take for the Titanic to sink?

A It took 2 hours and 40 minutes to sink

23

FAQ

THE ICEBERG & SINKING

 How many lifeboats were on the Titanic?

There were 16 lifeboats and 4 collapsible boats.

24

FAQ

THE ICEBERG & SINKING

 **How many people could fit in the first launched lifeboat?**

The first lifeboat could hold 65 people but left with only 28.

25

FAQ

THE ICEBERG & SINKING

Q What was the water temperature when the Titanic sank?

A

The water was around 28°F (-2°C)

26
FAQ
THE ICEBERG & SINKING

Q How many compartments were damaged?

A

Five compartments were flooded, which led to the sinking

27

FAQ

THE ICEBERG & SINKING

 How many people survived
the sinking?

About 710 people survived.

28

FAQ

Q

How many people did not survived the sinking?

A

About 1500 people did not survived the tragedy

29

FAQ

THE ICEBERG & SINKING

Q Did anything remain of the iceberg that sank the Titanic?

A Icebergs are made of freshwater and melt when they reach warmer waters. The iceberg that sank the Titanic likely melted within a few weeks after the collision.

30

FAQ

THE ICEBERG & SINKING

Q Was the iceberg always near where the Titanic sank?

A Actually, no! The iceberg was part of a glacier and had likely broken off from Greenland. It floated southward for months before crossing paths with the Titanic.

31

FAQ

AFTERMATH & LEGACY

 When was the wreckage of the Titanic found?

It was found on September 1, 1985

32

FAQ

AFTERMATH & LEGACY

Q How deep is the Titanic wreckage?

A It's about 12,500 feet (3,800 meters) below the surface.

33

FAQ

AFTERMATH & LEGACY

 **Q** Are there still Titanic survivors?

A The last living survivor, Millvina Dean, passed away in 2009. She was just two months old when she was on the Titanic.

34

FAQ

AFTERMATH & LEGACY

Q Is there a Titanic II?

A

There have been plans to build a modern-day replica of the Titanic, called Titanic II, but the plan was never completed.

35

FAQ

AFTERMATH & LEGACY

 **Q** Are people still searching for Titanic artifacts?

A

Yes, artifacts are still being recovered from the wreckage site. These items are often displayed in museums and exhibitions around the world.

36

FAQ

AFTERMATH & LEGACY

Q What happened to the lifeboats?

A

The lifeboats that were used to rescue survivors were originally left drifting in the ocean. Some were later recovered, but others are believed to have sunk or drifted away.

37

FAQ

AFTERMATH & LEGACY

 **Q** Did they ever try to raise the Titanic?

A

Many ideas have been proposed to raise the Titanic, but none have been successful. The depth, pressure, and fragile condition of the wreckage make it nearly impossible.

38

FAQ

AFTERMATH & LEGACY

Q How did they identify the Titanic at the bottom of the ocean?

A When the Titanic was found, a robotic submersible called "Jason Jr." explored the site and discovered the ship's boilers, which were uniquely identifiable as belonging to the Titanic.

39

FAQ

AFTERMATH & LEGACY

Q What happened to the captain?

A

Captain Edward Smith went down with the ship. His body was never found.

40
FAQ
RESCUE EFFORTS

Q How long did it take for the Carpathia to arrive?

A It took about four hours to reach the survivors

41

FAQ

RESCUE EFFORTS

 **Q** How far away was the Carpathia?

A

It was about 58 miles away when it received the distress signal

42

FAQ

RESCUE EFFORTS

Q

Was anyone pulled from the water alive?

A

Very few were pulled alive from the freezing water.

43

FAQ

 **Q** What did the Carpathia do with the survivors?

A The Carpathia took the survivors to New York City, which was the Titanic's original destination

44

FAQ

RESCUE EFFORTS

Q How did the Carpathia know that the Titanic was in trouble?

A

The Carpathia received a distress signal via wireless radio from the Titanic.

45

FAQ

RESCUE EFFORTS

Q Did the Carpathia receive any reward for the rescue?

A

Yes, the crew and Captain Arthur Rostron received medals and a silver cup from the Titanic survivors as a token of gratitude.

46

FAQ

THE JOURNEY

Q How fast could the Titanic go?

A

It could go up to 24 knots—
that's like going 28 miles
per hour on lan

47

FAQ

THE JOURNEY

Q Where did the Titanic set sail from?

A

It left from Southampton, England, aiming to reach New York City.

48

FAQ

THE JOURNEY

Q How long was the Titanic's estimated journey time

A The estimated journey time for the Titanic from Southampton, England to New York City, USA was about 7 days.

49

FAQ

THE JOURNEY

Q How many meals a day could First-Class passengers expect?

A

First-Class passengers could expect up to six meals a day, including lavish multi-course dinners.

50

FAQ

THE JOURNEY

Q

How many ports did the Titanic visit before heading to the Atlantic?

A

The Titanic visited two ports: Cherbourg, France, and Queenstown (now Cobh), Ireland.

51

FAQ

QUIZ TIME

 **Where was the Titanic built?**

A: In Belfast
B: in New York
C: in France

Answer is: A

52

FAQ

QUIZ TIME

Q

What year did the Titanic sink?

A

A: 1905
B: 1912
C: 1920

Answer is: B

53

FAQ

QUIZ TIME

Q How many smokestacks did the Titanic have?

A

A: 2
B: 4
C: 5

Answer is: B

54

FAQ

QUIZ TIME

Q

From which port did the
Titanic set sail?

A

A: New York
B: London
C: Southampton

Answer is: C

55

FAQ

QUIZ TIME

Q

What was the Titanic's final destination?

A

A: Tokyo
B: New York
C: Miami

Answer is: B

56

FAQ

QUIZ TIME

Q

How many classes of passengers were on the Titanic?

A

A: 3
B: 2
C: 4

Answer is: A

57

FAQ

QUIZ TIME

 On what date did the Titanic hit the iceberg?

A: April 14
B: April 12
C: July 4

Answer is: A

58

FAQ

QUIZ TIME

Q What was the name of the ship that rescued the survivors?

A

A: Lusitania
B: Queen Mary
C: Carpathia

Answer is: C

59

FAQ

QUIZ TIME

 Q How many lifeboats were on the Titanic?

A

A: 28
B: 14
C: 20

Answer is: C

60
FAQ
QUIZ TIME

Q Who was the captain of the Titanic?

A

A: Edward Smith
B: James Cook
C: Jack Sparrow

Answer is: A

61

FAQ

QUIZ TIME

 How many people survived the sinking of the Titanic?

A: 706
B: 1500
C: 1023

Answer is: A

62

FAQ

QUIZ TIME

Q **Where is the Titanic wreckage located?**

A

A: Pacific Ocean
B: Indian Ocwean
C: Atlantic Ocean

Answer is: C

63

FAQ

QUIZ TIME

 **Q** How long did it take to build the Titanic?

A

A: 5 Years

B: 2 Years

C:3 Years

Answer is: C

64

FAQ

QUIZ TIME

Q How many people worked on building the Titanic?

A

A: Around 5,000
B: Around 3,000
C: More than 10,000

Answer is: B

65

FAQ

QUIZ TIME

Q How far away was the Carpathia when it received the distress signal from the Titanic?

A

A: 58 miles
B: 107 miles
C: over 150 miles

Answer is: A

66

FAQ

QUIZ TIME

Q What was the most expensive first-class suite price (in today's money)?

A

A: $75,000
B: $100,000
C: $50,000

Answer is: B

67

FAQ

QUIZ TIME

Q In what year was the wreck of the Titanic discovered?

A

A: 1965

B: 1985

C: 1997

Answer is: B

68

FAQ

QUIZ TIME

Q How deep is the water where the Titanic sank?

A

A: 2,500 feet
B: 20,000 feet
C: 12,500 feet

Answer is: C

69

FAQ

QUIZ TIME

Q How long did it take for the Titanic to sink after hitting the iceberg?

A

A: Less than an hour
B: 4 hours
C: 2 hours and 40 minutes

Answer is: C

70

FAQ

QUIZ TIME

Q

How many meals a day could a first-class passenger expect?

A

A: 3
B: 6
C: 8

Answer is: B

71

FAQ

QUIZ TIME

 **Q** How old was the youngest survivor of the Titanic?

A

A: 6 months
B: 2 years
C: 2 months

Answer is: C

72

FAQ

QUIZ TIME

Q

How many distress rockets did the Titanic fire to signal for help?

A

A: 12
B: 18
C: 8

Answer is: A

73

FAQ

QUIZ TIME

Q What year did the Titanic movie starring Leonardo DiCaprio and Kate Winslet release?

A

A: 1990

B: 1997

C: 1995

Answer is: B

74

FAQ

QUIZ TIME

 **Q** What was the top speed of the Titanic?

A

A: 35 knots
B: 10 knots
C: 23 knots

Answer is: C

75

FAQ

QUIZ TIME

 How heavy was the Titanic when fully loaded?

A: 65,128 tons
B: 52,310 tons
C: 45,400 tons

Answer is: B

76

FAQ

QUIZ TIME

Q How many miles is the sea distance from Southampton to New York City?

A

A: 2,500 miles
B: 4,000 miles
C: 3,450 miles

Answer is: C

77

FAQ

QUIZ TIME

Q How many miles had the Titanic traveled from Southampton until it hit the iceberg?

A

A: About 1,191 miles
B: About 800 miles
C: About 1,500 miles

Answer is: A

BOOK REVIEW

★ ★ ★ ★ ★

Hello my Friend

If you've enjoyed our journey through this book and found it beneficial for sparking curiosity and joy in your child's learning, I'd deeply appreciate it if you could leave a review.

Your feedback not only supports my work but also aids in collaborating with other publishers to create engaging and educational content for our children.

If you liked this book, you'll be happy to know I have recommendations for similar enriching reads your kids will love too. Sharing your thoughts through a review can help more families discover the joy of learning together. Thank you for your support and for joining us on this adventure

William Anchor

AMAZON BOOK RECOMMENDATION

Mind Challengers: Difficult Riddles for Super Smart Kids

 ★★★★★ **CHECKOUT** 🛒 **Age: 6-12**

MIND CHALLENGERS

OVER 300 MIND CHALLENGING RIDDLES FOR YOUNG GENIES

BRAIN TEASERS THAT KIDS AND FAMILIES WILL LOVE

DIFFICULT RIDDLES FOR SUPER SMART KIDS

300 RIDDLES

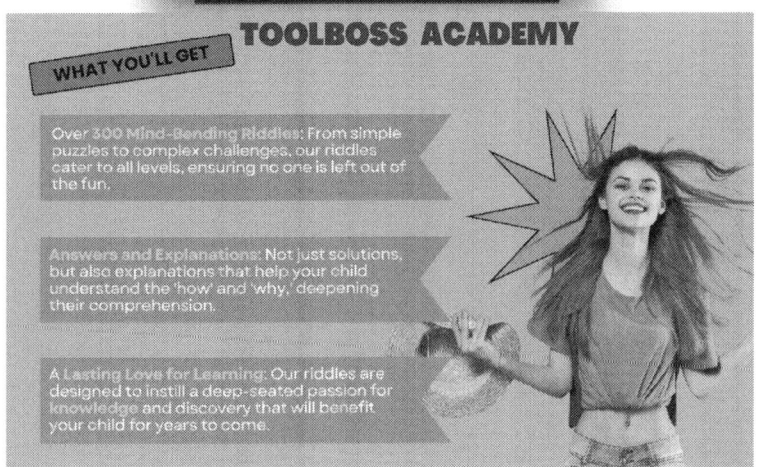

TOOLBOSS ACADEMY

WHAT YOU'LL GET

Over 300 Mind-Bending Riddles: From simple puzzles to complex challenges, our riddles cater to all levels, ensuring no one is left out of the fun.

Answers and Explanations: Not just solutions, but also explanations that help your child understand the 'how' and 'why,' deepening their comprehension.

A Lasting Love for Learning: Our riddles are designed to instill a deep-seated passion for knowledge and discovery that will benefit your child for years to come.

AMAZON BOOK RECOMMENDATION

Brain Sparker: Explaining the Fascinating Secrets of Our World in History and Science

Age: 8-16

Made in United States
Troutdale, OR
01/25/2025